3

Murano. Glass Museum, water vase.

Caposil

Venice, Lido Beach.

Chioggia. Fisherman.

San Lazzaro. The Armenians' Island.

Preganziòl

Mogliano Veneto

Marcon

Zero
Zero
Mogliano V.to
Oese
Dese
Mestre Est

Zelarino
Castellana
Fávaro Veneto

Mirano
Spinea
Via Miranese
Campalto
Tessera

MESTRE

Chirignago

Ca' Sabbioni
Mestre Ovest
Can. d. Osellino

P.to Marghera
P.te d. Libertà
Murano
S. Erasmo

Malcontenta
S. Michele
Le Vignole

Fusina
VENEZIA

La Giudecca

San Clemente
S. Lazzaro

Sacca Sessola
Lido

Bacino di Malamocco
Malamocco

Porto di S. Leonardo
Alberoni

Valle Dell'Averto

S. Maria d. Mare

Valle del Cornio
S. Pietro in Volta

Porto Secco

Valle Fossa della Magra
S. Antonio

Pellestrina

Bacino di Chioggia

Caroman

Valli
CHIOGGIA

Strada Romea

Bacchiglione Brenta

Valle di Brenta

SOTTOMARINA

Porto di Chioggia

Lido di Sottomarina

a Romea

Brenta

Aereoporto
Marco Polo

Torcello
Palude dei Traja
Lio Piccolo

Burano
Caval

Treporti
Ca Ballarin

Punta Sabbioni
Ca Savio

Litorale del Cavallin

Porto di Lido

Litorale di Lido

MARE ADRIATICO

Porto di Malamocco

Litorale di Pellestrina

LAGUNA

VENETA

Maggiore
Ca di Va

Venice Lagoon

MURANO • BURANO • TORCELLO • JESOLO • PUNTA SABBIONI • LIDO

135 COLOUR ILLUSTRATIONS • 5 MAPS

Seascape, Venice lagoon-sunset.

STORTI EDIZIONI

A View of the lagoon.

D oes it matter exactly when we set out on our Lagoon itinerary?

The alchemy of countless possible factors, such as a fresh and sparkling summer morning, a limpid autumn with a hint of distant storm, the encounter of multifarious refractions of light with the languid and silent water of the shoals, will contribute to the sensations that will probably remain with us forever. We may find ourselves chained to fragmentary revelations of centuries-old history or intangible moments of poetic melancholy.

What will be our most memorable impression? Perhaps the first amazing impact of being in such a unique place, or a gradually mounting sensation of echo and symmetry between the rhythm of daily life and the rise and fall of the waters. Or perhaps our final surrender to a passionate interest that becomes ever more enthralling and inescapable.

Before we start, however, we can be certain that, like an attack of double vision, any impressions and images we may possibly gain of Venice will be overlaid and confused by our prior knowledge and by our imagination. They will even be affected to some extent by the means of transport that we use at various times, whether we board a calm and punctual but rather clumsily shaped and down-at-heel waterbus, or a darting modern speedboat, all waves and splashes, together with rushed and astonished tourists. Shall we pry about in a small motorboat or slide silently in on the tip of an oar? Or shall we treat ourselves to the rare luxury of a gondola?

It matters little. Venice and her lagoon have for centuries aroused strong and contradictory passions of pride and loyalty, jealousy, resentment and rivalry, artistic inspiration, fascination and ecstasy, so it is unlikely that they will at any moment begrudge their unassuming modern visitors unforgettable emotions, nor fail to find a lasting home in their hearts.

The precariousness of the present time, the erosion by natural agents and men's neglect sometimes induce pessimism, but Venice can give immediate reassurance with a display of unequalled splendours from the past that, in spite of the odds, survive in such number that history is encountered at every step.

It is probably this, this extraordinary past that emerges and then withdraws like the flow of a tide at every attempt to discover the present or envisage the future, that binds all incurable devotees of Venice and her sea.

The lagoon near the mainland.

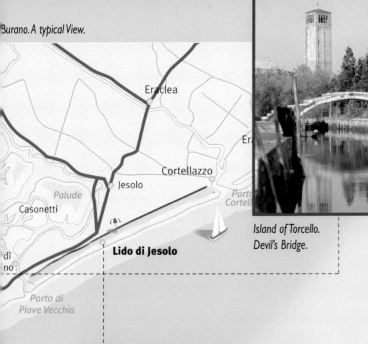

Burano. A typical View.

*Island of Torcello.
Devil's Bridge.*

Jesolo Lido. The Lighthouse.

Murano

T he motorship we have boarded at Fondamenta Nuove has hooted its imminent departure. The dull roar of the propellers pops into a noisy churning of foam, which spreads out like the fan of a peacock while the thick ropes uncurl from the bollards. We are atop the weather deck, from where we can admire the ample sweep of the lagoon, crossed to our right by the Ponte Lagunare.

We point the prow towards the Island of Murano and skim fleetingly alongside the Rio dei Gesuiti.

A traveller of the last century would have emerged from this same canal aboard a "gondola-omnibus" caught at the "stazio" a little further on, near the Palazzo Morosini, on whose façade were to be admired the remains of frescoes by Veronese, and famous for its garden stocked with statues and exotic animals.

On the ferry colonnade a boatman has left us the written record of the day when he walked to Murano on foot, in a winter when the lagoon was completely frozen over. During his unusual walk he will certainly have rested at the first large island of San Cristoforo della Pace, later joined to the adjacent island of San Michele, when the cemetery arrangements were more rationally replanned in 1837.

In the livid pallor of the lagoon, the serene and

Murano Glass.

softly rounded shape of the Church of San Michele, early embryo of Codussi's major splendours, will certainly not have appeared to his ignorant eyes as a delicate flower of Renaissance architecture, but as a reassuring exhortation to continue his walk to the nearby Church of Santa Maria degli Angeli on Murano, where the Ferrymen's School, the "Scola dei Barcajuoli", to which he belonged honoured Saint Christopher as their protector.

When Santa Maria degli Angeli was rebuilt in the 16th century it gazed at its solitary reflection in the lagoon, surrounded by rich vegetation that hid, like a water lily, its vast and famous adjoining monastery. Here Giacomo Casanova came, not very devoutly, to meet a nun whose name he discreetly withholds, though not her carnal virtues.

The Island of Murano used to be a succession of vegetable fields, vineyards and gardens, the delights whereof were praised by Andrea Calmo. It would be hard today, among the picturesque fashionable meetingpoints and cultured literary academies, the busy glass factories and seventeen serene churches, to trace the ancient layout of the hospices

Island of San Michele. The small cloister.

Church of S. Michele. Façade.

Pag. 8/9 Murano. Air view.

and many convents that once existed. Of this beauty, all derived from the lagoon, and formerly defended by a specific autonomy and particular administrative privileges, there remain only sporadic traces. Its delightful gardens having vanished from view, Murano now perpetuates its ancient beauty only in the art of glasswork.

The gondola from which Carlo Gozzi furtively landed here with an attractive lady neighbour of his - one of his few youthful loves and very soon thwarted - would have had much ado to keep its balance amid the washes of fast tourist speedboats dashing incessantly to and from the glassworkers' landing-stages.

Murano. Glass work.

Let us explore the fascinating dens reached by way of corridors jumbled with bales of straw and fragrant firwood packing-cases, and crucibles that spit fire through narrow slits. At the end of iron rods, small blobs of incandescent glass whirl through the air from the furnace to the "piazza", the place where the "maestro" works. A picturesque dance proceeds with phrased and rhythmic movements over a monody of primitive sounds, until the moment when a decisive puff turns the fiery mass into a fine, transparent bubble which takes on various colours as it cools, while being modelled into an animal, a vase, a flower, a bowl, a tumbler, a cruet or any one of a thousand articles emerging uniquely from the imagination

and skill of their creator.

This fine glass leaf is, in a way, a basic and emblematic key for understanding the feeling of Venice, her lagoon and her light. It is a fragile thing, surprisingly and unnaturally lightweight, frail, beautiful in its delicate arabesques and, in fact, rare in its progressive unity.

The history of glasswork and many splendid examples of it are displayed in the Palazzo Giustiniani, former residence of the Bishops of Torcello and since 1861 the home of the Museo Vetrario (Glass Museum). Repeated study and contemplation can help us to perceive more closely the refinement of a society which, although essentially mercantile, did not neglect to embellish the regular occasions of daily life with tasteful and simple glassware, widely commissioned by public, private and religious patrons.

The fascinating objects of glass and network filigree, the splendid multicoloured enamels, the engraved decorations, the milk-scabs that counterfeited porcelain, the glass stained to imitate precious stone, the translucent murrhines of ancient

Murano. Works of art.

Roman tradition or the aventurines with their golden iridescence lead us to a better comprehension of the palette of colours that makes up the luminosity of the lagoon.

We reach the Museo Vetrario by walking along Fondamenta dei Vetrai and across the long Ponte Vivarini, crossing the island's own "Grand Canal", turning our backs on the Palazzo Da Mula with its Veneto-Byzantine echoes and melancholy state of dilapidation. After the Museum, the Venetian origins emerge from the solitary survival of the Basilica of Santa Maria and Donato, one of the many

Pag. 12 Murano, Basilica of Santa Maria and Donato.

Murano. Fondamenta Cavour. Murano. Belfry and church of Santo Stefano.

churches that were built on the lagoon after the year 1000. The outer architecture of its apse together with the remains of mosaic paving inside form an introduction to the remote and solitary remains on Torcello, which is our next goal.

We can barely make out the distant outline of its belfry and the ample curve of the basilica facing the lagoon, which suddenly opens out before our eyes as, aboard a kindly available boat that happened to be passing, we come out of the Canale di San Matteo, which takes its name from a convent built on the initiative of a group of Venetian noble-

women who lived under the Benedictine order towards the end of the 13th century.

The next stop on the tour may be either Torcello or Burano.

The visit to Torcello can be comfortably planned to catch one of a number of connections to Burano.

Those wishing to visit the Island of Burano first are advised to alight at the Mazzorbo stop and continue on foot, thus profiting from a delightful walk.

For those wishing to go first to Murano there are connections from Fondamenta Nuove every 10-15 minutes throughout the day. In this case it is advisable to use Line 5. When Murano has been seen, those wishing to go on to Burano or Torcello should go to the stop "Faro".

Murano. Lagoon view.

Murano: Lighthouse, air view.

THINGS TO SEE

Santa Maria degli Angeli

Basilica of Santa Maria and Donato

Glass museum

Church of San Pietro Martire

MURANO

Palude del Monte

Canale di S. Maria

Canale degli Angeli

Canale degli Angeli

Canale Ondello

Canale dei Marani

Campo Sportivo

Cimitero Nuovo

Cimitero

Sacca Serenella

SERENELLA

VENIER

Pal. Da Mula

Campo S. Stefano

Campo S. Donato

Palazzo Trevisan

NAVAGERO

MURANO FARO

COLONNA

SAN MICHELE ISLAND

Church of San Michele.
*(1469-70 Architect Mauro Codussi)
Prototype of the Renaissance church in Venice. Beside the church is the Emilian Chapel (1530) built by*

CIMITERO

Cimitero San Michele

1 *Church of San Michele. Interior.*

1 *Church of San Michele.*

Guglielmo Bergamasco on a hexagonal plan and in Lombard style.
In 1560 some restoration was carried out by Jacopo Sansovino.
The Venetian-Gothic belfry with fired brick decoration was brought to completion in 1460.
A small 14th-century inner cloister is reached through a portal surmounted by a Gothic cusp and a sculpture representing St Michael slaying the Dragon.

2 CHURCH OF SAN PIETRO MARTIRE

(Parish) The structure assumed its present form in 1511 after the rebuilding and extension of an earlier church and adjoining convent founded by the Dominican Fathers in 1348. When Napoleon decreed the dissolution of the convents it was entirely stripped of its artistic assets. The present ones come from other religious buildings on the island that were dissolved or destroyed in the last century. Inside are canvases by Jacopo Palma the Younger and others attributed to Giovanni Bellini, Jacopo Tintoretto and the school of Titian. There is an interesting painting of "The Marriage in Cana" by B. Letterini (1669-1745) with the diners in period costume, also the group of musicians.
Of great interest are the wooden panels in the Sacristy.

3 BASILICA OF SANTA MARIA AND DONATO

Rebuilt on an earlier construction apparently dating from the 7th century, it assumed its present form in 1140 and is a most eminent example of Veneto-Byzantine style, its architectural perfection harmonising with a variety of decorative features in the apse section. Marco Giustiniani, a wealthy nobleman elected bishop of the diocese in 1692, contributed certain "improvements" which, through too much devotion and ignorance, unfortunately caused enor-

3 *Basilica and campanile of Santa Maria and Donato.*

3 *Basilica of Santa Maria and Donato. Symbolic figures in mosaic.*

*mous impairment and dispersal of valuable medievals. In the 19th century, intensive restoration work was undertaken, culminating in recent operations during 1973-79, which restored some of the original ancient fineries.
Noteworthy are the mosaic pavements interspersed with geometric motifs and animal figures, and particularly the great mosaic of the Virgin at Prayer, which entirely covers the apse ceiling.*

4 S. MARIA DEGLI ANGELI

The church stands alone at the end of the Fondamenta Venier, enclosed by a few remnants of walling and surrounded by a small lawn. It used to have a vast adjoining monastery, but was rebuilt in the 16th century and subsequently tampered with, the nuns' choir abolished and the front part designated as a lazar house. Nevertheless, the Baroque interior, including the sectioned ceiling painted by Pennacchi, is not lacking in singular charm. On the walls are interesting works by Jacopo Palma the Younger, Antonio Pordenone and Salviati.

5 GLASS MUSEUM

The entrance vestibule is strewn with marble remains from various periods, recovered from sundry places on the island. In the upper rooms visitors can follow the fascinating history of glass-making from archaeological displays with finds from excavations down to present-day products.

Burano

Burano. Lace boutique.

'I nfin ch'el tempo è belo /
As long as the weather is fine
andemo a far bordelo / let's kick
up a shindy andemo a ciassisar /
let's go and make a din puti ga-
lanti / amorous lads. Montemo el
bateleto/ let's get on a boat mar-
ciemo col frescheto / let's walk in
the cool evening metemose a so-
nar / let's make music femo fra-
casso / let's make a racket.

This is an old 18th century
"canzone da bateo" (boat song), whose German com-
poser Johann Adolf Hasse, popularly known as "the Sax-
on", probably got his inspiration here in Burano when
visiting his colleague Baldassare Galuppi, then engrossed
in setting to music a comic opera by that other fine wit,
Carlo Goldoni.

The more striking and showy Burano is the ideal
goal for a boat trip. Here the gay, rustic mood of a
cheerful crowd culminates in a mounting din of con-
viviality, perhaps at the end of its enthusiastic regatta,
which is held on the third Sunday in September and
finishes with the crowds pouring into the wide central
piazza amid the savoury smell of gigantic polentas and
crisp fried fish.

But like everything on
the lagoon, this island too
has its hidden identity, the
reverse of the other. For
Burano is also an individu-
al discovery, solitary and
extremely personal. It
makes sentimental over-
tures that one becomes
aware of with trepidation

while drawing ever close, first
discovering the attenuated
abandon of a faded water-
colour then from nearer, the
colourful, irrational vivacity of
its houses. The lagoon's lonely,
dreamy peace like a painting by
Carpaccio, as seen when
rounding the church of Santa
Caterina of Mazzorbo, is soon
unexpectedly shattered by a
piece of picturesque imperti-
nence: its whimsical leaning belfry swerving skywards.

He who does not know Burano does not know the
light of the lagoon. At the end of the last century it was
here in Burano that the Italian Impressionists succeeded in capturing and rendering on canvas the luminous
refractions peculiar to out-of-doors painting. While Venice, as though in another hemisphere, declined with
complacency into her own myth in the early 20th century, Burano seemed to incarnate a new symbol of life
in the pictorial illusion of its luminosity. From Moggioli
to Gino Rossi, from Semeghini to Dalla Zorza onwards,
there is no artist who has not sketched something
among Burano's fields, shores and canals, but found himself more or less incapable
of grasping the colour of its
lagoon; half a century earlier, Camillo Boito had de-
scribed it as ineffable.

A great part of the
inhabitants' daily life also
takes place out of doors.
They are fishermen in ori-

Burano. Picturesque corner.

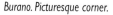

Pag20/21. Burano. Air view.

Burano. Lace makers.

gin, and it is only a short step from their boats to their houses. In the street, near to their front doors, they still perform customs and chores belonging to ancient communal life, the comic "ciacole" (ditties) chanted in a melodious dialect, the boat cleaning, the net mending, the popping embers in their ingenious stoves for cooking fish, the lace making on drums hugged on the laps of the oldest women. These are authentic images of former times, a little faded of course, but still preserving their own genuine island grace, even though we can no longer see them against the background of kitchens gleaming with beaten copper or platters of golden fritters on sooty hearths.

From the centre of the piazza small arcades and colourful lanes survey, like wide-eyed children the enchantment of the lagoon entirely surrounding the island.

We pull away slowly in a fisherman's boat, smelling of salt and sundried seaweed.

Burano. Torso: Baldassare Galuppi.
Background: Lace school.

Houses, canals, and lagoon life.

Ex Batteria Mazzorbo

Canale di Mazzorbo

Fondamenta di Santa Caterina

Canale di Burano

Palude del Monte

Strada del Cimitero

Fond. di Santa Caterina

BURANO

Corte Comare

2 Lace museum

3 Church of S. Martino

Palude di Burano

1 Church of S. Caterina

Palude di S. Caterina

---

1 MAZZORBO - LITTLE CHURCH OF SANTA CATERINA

In 14th-century Romanesque-Gothic style, it maintains the appearance of an early 15th-century chapel. It had an adjoining convent of nuns, but that was dissolved in the 19th-century. The keel roof, characteristic of other Venetian churches, is one of the few examples of its kind remaining in lagoon territory. At the end of the Mazzorbo Canal, before the wooden bridge that joins it with Burano, stands the picturesque bell tower, recently cleaned and restored, which is the only surviving remnant of the vanished convent of Santa Maria di Valverde.

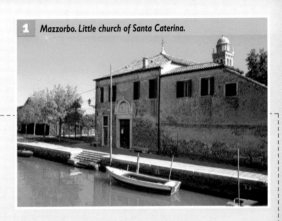

1 *Mazzorbo. Little church of Santa Caterina.*

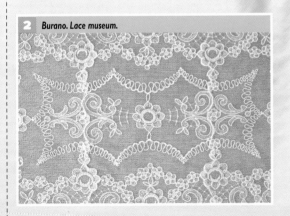

2 *Burano. Lace museum.*

2 BURANO - LACE MUSEUM

Fine and valuable examples of this world-famous art.

3 BURANO - CHURCH OF SAN MARTINO

A 15th-century building in the form of a Latin cross with three naves, holding some mementoes of the island's history and art.

Torcello

ISLAND OF THE ORIGINS

Canale Bisatto.

We set sail - or would if we were lucky - towards Torcello, and here that idea of lagoon that we formed while seeing Venice and observing it both from the canals and from the wide panorama of St Mark's Basin suddenly becomes elusive and indefinable.

At the beginning of the winding Canale del Bisatto (Eel) the lagoon opens out in its more natural and primitive essence in which, on the distant line of the horizon, the meeting of sky and water becomes merely a mental abstraction.

To the left our gaze is lost as far as the edge of the mainland, while to the right it is framed by thin streaks of ochre-coloured sandbank surmounted, in perspective, by distant groups of trees from which jut occasional chimneys and a few belfries. What mysterious discoveries await us?

The slow approach to Torcello, sidling by the derelict and still deteriorating remains of the islands of San Giacomo in Paludo and Madonna del Monte, arouses a profound sensation of a return to the origins— not only to those of the first nucleus of settlers who sought shelter from the 6th-century Barbarian invasions and who here, between a flourishing, essentially maritime economic vocation and a stuttering residential development,

began to give shape and awareness to what was to become the Duchy of Venice, but also to the primordial origins of marginal life connected with the trade routes coming along Roman roads that were obliged to carry their oil and wine across the waters of the lagoon in order to reach Istria.

Torcello, with its surrounding lands and the engulfing waters that penetrate it like the veins of a human body, with its cultivated isles and its desert stretches, the sea eroding its shores in a maternal frenzy to inhale its essential oxygen from them, the immense sky looming over all, embracing all, reflecting from the water the light that it itself radiates, has the very same beauty as that of an ancient landscape. It is the same as that of which we find delicate evidence as early as 537 in the report by Cassiodorus, minister of the Gothic King Vitiges, who has left us an account saying between irony and amazement that "*the boats appear tied to the houses like domestic animals, where the unstable terrain is protected from the assault of the billows by means of interwoven withies. The houses look like marsh birds' nests and the boats pulled up on land by means of ropes seem to be drifting round the meadows*"

No trace now remains of the refound serenity of the Roman population

Torcello. The Cathedral amidst the barene.

who embarked at the ports of Altino to seek refuge in the sinuous recesses of the lagoon from the barbaric violence of the Huns and the Lombards, nor of the consequent prosperity and dominion. The ancient events of a flourishing and busy city, rich in villas, churches, convents and palaces are nothing but a memory bordering on legend.

In spite of the noisy spate of tourists, ebbing and flowing according to the season, its internationally famed inn, and its delightfully fragrant orchards now recovered from the malaria that still existed about a century ago, Torcello is at present a valuable archaeological repository enclosed in agonizing solitude. Its cathedral, dedicated to Santa Maria Assunta, is the most ancient surviving Veneto-Byzantine building in the lagoons. The characteristic salient form of its belfry softens, as it descends, into the rotundity of its apses and the porticoes of the adjacent church of Santa Fosca.

Torcello. The Campanile of the Cathedral.
Torcello. A hut.
Torcello. The municipal palace.

Torcello. Church of Santa Fosca.

Torcello. Little square.

Torcello. Expanse facing the Locanda Cipriani.

Torcello. Well head.

It is a place that should be approached little by little, slowly, in a roundabout way, as in the outer corridors of a labyrinth; an ultimate goal that vanishes and reappears with the windings of the journey. We land there already tainted by the discreet charm of the sandbanks, where we have progressively learned to listen to the silence.

We have sailed over sedimentations of history and millenarian sands, passing the Isle of Ammiana, a Byzantine Atlantis swallowed up by the marsh mud, and nearing the Ossuary of Sant'Ariano with its impassable jungle of ruins overflowing its ancient walls. We have crossed abandoned saltworks from which timid little white herons took off in flight, skirted muddy marshland at the mouths of rivers, and ploughed through canals shaded by huge trawlnets supported in the trickle of water by enormously long arms stretching skywards like the spans of a Gothic cathedral, incrusted with the white droppings of perching seagulls.

Torcello is, above all, an abstraction on the threshold of history, which in the end is better understood by climbing its solitary belfry and looking out of its mullioned windows to observe in its entirety the alternation and blending of water, sea and sky that we know as the Venice Lagoon. The rest is archaeological remains, anecdote and curiosity that intersect and pursue each other among the marble decorations and mosaics of the Cathedral, the few remnants of the Baptistry dating from the 7th century, and a marble chair that legend claims to be the throne of Attila the Hun. It is a solitary little village on whose walls, in overlapping fragments, centuries of Byzantine history can be read.

The church square is enlivened by the typical and picturesque touristic enterprises, with a few stalls selling lace and glassware, which rather overshadow a notice board that, with its tolls and boatmen's fees, brings us back to a commercial reality less conducive to contemplative abandon.

Let us return to our boat.

Along the narrow street that flanks the canal and the picturesque Ponte del Diavolo (Devil's Bridge) without parapets, like the old Venetian bridges where youths from rival quarters would hold fisticuffs battles, the silence of the lagoon that has driven us as far as this island of the past is shattered by an increasingly vivacious and contagious burst of chatter.

Ahead appears Burano in all its pert, brash colours.

Torcello. Devil's Bridge.

Torcello. Attila's throne.

Canale Borgognoni

Fondamenta dei Borgognoni

1 Cathedral of S. Maria Assunta

2 Church of Santa Fosca

TORCELLO

BURANO

1 Torcello. Piazzetta and the Cathedral and the Church of Santa Fosca.

1 CATHEDRAL OF SANTA MARIA ASSUNTA

An 11th-century Veneto-Byzantine building, an example of Romanesque evolution of the Ravenna church type. Opposite the façade are a few remains of the 7th-century Baptistry. Of interest on the side of the church are the large hinged stone slabs used to close the windows. Inside is a wooden ceiling and mosaic floor with geometric motifs. Presbytery choir and iconostasis (screen of 15th-century panels showing the Virgin and the 12 Apostles). Of great interest are the mosaics in the middle of the apse, a row of Apostles surmounted by a Madonna Teothòkos (Mother of God). Opposite, above the main door, is a stupendous mosaic depicting the Apotheosis of Christ and the Last Judgement.

1 Cathedral of Santa Maria Assunta. Presbytery.

Torcello. Archaeological Funds.

2 CHURCH OF SANTA FOSCA

Standing next to the Cathedral, it was built in the 11th-12th century and echoes oriental schemes with an interior in the form of a Greek cross and three naves, and an octagonal exterior ringed on five sides by a portico with Veneto-Byzantine capitals.

The barene around Torcello.

Lagoon Landscape

Burano can be considered the hub of the lagoon's most beautiful and pleasing part. From here, spreading out in an evocative ellipse, is the great sense of history that emanates from the neighbouring Torcello, the ascetic silence of San Francesco del Deserto a few oarstrokes away, then a wide expanse that divides and breaks up into a succession of sweet little islands, minute outcrops with eroded shores and golden sandbanks, curled up around canals caressed by the slow ebb and flow of the tides. With its fragmented and rapid succession of small beaches, anchored in the water by the finest of marsh canes, it is a place that knows no horizon and therefore, with its ready havens, not even the anguish of silence and solitude.

Here, more than in any other place on the lagoon, we find ourselves in the centre of the brackish ecosystem generated by the state of fragile and precarious symbiosis between the fresh water of the rivers and the salt water of the sea. In contrast to the marsh fauna and the morphological and vegetable formations that mutate according to the combination of the two fundamental factors that generate this lagoon environment, the "culture" of the human settlements of Venice rests on the ability of her ancient inhabitants to control the variability of these characteristics.

Created by the confluence of river and sea water, the lagoons would tend to vanish into the ground in the course of natural evolution, by the very action of their own generative phenomena.

The survival of Venice as a city today is due to the action of her governments who, in an age-old struggle, diverted rivers, protected the shores and reinforced the beaches, bending nature's normal evolution to their own advantage. The environment of the Venice lagoon has therefore an indissoluble organic identity as marvellous as it is precarious, in which the mutual influence of history and nature is the main characteristic of its cultural synthesis.

Our boat is long and flat, suitable for shallow waters. Formerly a firearm would have been mounted on it for lagoon shooting in the days when wild duck and coot could be bagged even with bow and arrow, as we can see from paintings by Pietro Longhi. Slowly leaving Torcello and Sant'Ariano on the right, and taking advantage of the high tide, we pass the white island of Santa Cristina. The topography is enriched by names appropriate to the natural conformations of the la-

Pag. 40/41. San Francesco del deserto.

goon, marsh, islet, vale, salt-flats and so on, where we find, all the same, the comforting signs of man's presence.

This is one of the many independent places where fishing activity survives, albeit with increasing difficulty. We skirt an area where the fishermen have cast their nets, enclosing a wide square of water,

then follow the rudimentary signs on poles sunk into the mud to indicate the deeper water, and arrive at the end of the Canale di San Felice. Our long excursion has reserved another enchanting surprise.

Enclosed between small shoaly beaches, we find a picturesque fishing settlement rising on the waterline, just a row of huts built of any chance material, the poor man's architecture, with piles of articles and utensils for work. Alongside the minute canals are raised the "vieri" (crab pots), the large baskets where the crabs complete their mutation cycle, while on the banks dogs start to bark instinctively, but promptly crave a pat when the boat lands. A little way off the nets are stretched to dry, twisted round slim poles surmounted by small resting gulls, and as they sway in the sun they cast a delicate embroidery of light and shade.

Our slow return, facilitated by the turn of the tide,

Views of the Lagoon.

brings us back near to Burano, to the island of San Francesco del Deserto, where a straight line of shimmering green cypresses announces the presence of the one remaining monastic residence on the lagoon together with San Lazzaro degli Armeni.

A grassy avenue leads us to a small entrance where the sound of a bell debars us from the serene hospitality of the few friars who live and work here, perpetuating the testimony of a legend that claims that Saint Francis of Assisi rested in this place.

Fortunately our oarsman knows every secret depth of this corner of paradise inch by inch. Instead of rowing back the way we came, we turn left and carry on round the island until, through a small aperture between two strips of sand, our prow points out the Island of Sant'Erasmo ahead.

In a warning notice that still hangs on a door of Palazzo dei Camerlenghi in Rialto, beside the herb market, can be read one of the few official references to this island, otherwise totally and inexplicably ignored by any reference whatsoever beyond a simple mention.

"His Most Serene Highness the Prince makes known ... that it is the resolute and firm intention of His Excellency ... that the vegetable growers of Chioza, Pelestrina, Malamoco, Santo Erasmo, Vignole, Zuecca, Lido and Tre Porti, who come to sell in this city ... in the places appointed ... may dispose with all confidence of the goods that they carry for the city's universal benefit and convenience..."

The inscription is valuable because, amongst other things, it provides a detailed map of the areas of Venice that were once agricultural. Of the above list, only the areas of Sant'Erasmo and Vignole still find a total commercial outlet in the Rialto market, while the others have almost or completely disappeared, either because housing development has obliterated their an-

Belfry, San Francesco del deserto.

The Market Gardens of Sant'Erasmo.

cient market gardens, or because the tourist industry has more recently taken over their economy. The large island of Sant'Erasmo and the adjacent Vignole now remain the most luxuriant market gardens in Venice, famous for their fine-tasting early vegetables such as artichokes, asparagus, peas and aubergines, which once used to be carried to Venice by rowing boat, where they were greeted with cheerful and colourful jubilation when they passed along the city's canals in the afternoon.

Sant'Erasmo has no ancient relics, with the exception of a few interesting boundary stones, to bring it within the realm of tourist interest, but it has the beauty and personality of the countryside, with the attraction of quiet, shady walks, the long stretch of market gardens, the rows of vines, the

Lagoon Lights.

fields of flowers, the orchards and the local sparkling wine. It is a mainland in the middle of the sea, making it, in related socio-economic matters, an absolute anomaly in the context of lagoon problems.

There are three stops on Sant'Erasmo: Capannone, Chiesa and Punta Vela, any one of which may serve as the point of departure for a walk round the island, which should take about two hours. It is advisable, however, to stop at Capannone and go along the avenue opposite as far as a little beach which commands a wide panorama of the Fort of Sant'Andrea at the very end of San Nicolò del Lido and the entrance to the Porto del Lido. Continuing either for a short way along the beach or by inland road, you arrive at the small town of Chiesa, from where you can enjoy a splendid view of Burano before going on to Punta Vela.

Sant'Erasmo offers the charm of a country ramble among the lagoon's market gardens. There are

no restaurants on the island, just a couple of refreshment stands by the beach, and as a rule these only function in summer. The choice seems to lie between taking a packed lunch or stopping to eat at Vignole, where, especially on weekdays, one may enjoy a meal in complete peace under the shade of the tamarisks and oleanders.

The Island of San Francesco del Deserto cannot be reached by public transport. A visit to it is included in some tours offered by tourist agencies. With a little luck it is possible to contract a ferry from Burano with some local old gondolier.

Lagoon fisherman.

The Lido

W e skirt the Island of San Erasmo on the side facing the adjacent Lazzaretto Nuovo, where once all crews suspected of infectious diseases had to stay in quarantine, and emerge into the wide panorama of the entrance to the Porto del Lido.

We leave behind our erstwhile impressions, as we are suddenly struck by new ones. The mighty fortress of Sant'Andrea, built in 1543 by the architect Michele Sanmichele, jolts us into the military Venice, "for the glory of our Lion" as sang the Venetians who concentrated their defensive strategy on this naval fortress.

Opposite the Sant'Andrea fortification there used to be another at San Nicolò at the far eastern end of the Lido; old 16th-century maps, in fact, refer to "two castles". It was from here that the noble Doge would emerge on his gilded barge, the Bucintoro, for the cerimony of his wedding to the sea, and here the Venetian government, with all pomp, received illustrious guests.

Thirty thousand crusaders stayed at this end of the Lido in 1202, preparing to depart on the Crusade; like certain highly successful films today, this performance had reached its fourth edition. The episode is worth mentioning to show the totally non-religious acumen of the Venetians. The crusaders were late in paying for their transport to the

Holy Land, so the Doge persuaded their captains to go first to Dalmatia and conquer the city of Jadera (now Zadar), which Hungary had seized from Venice, and make this enterprise satisfy a large part of the agreed payment. The campaign proved convenient for including Constantinople on the "tour" too, and the iniquitous sack that ensued has no parallel in history. A treasure chest filled over nine centuries opened as if by magic and, to give an idea of the scale of the affair, suffice it to recall that the Treasure of Saint Mark and the Horses that grace his Basilica derive from that celebrated "victory", while the Sainte-Chapelle in Paris was built expressly to house the French share of the booty.

With the decline of its military and civil functions, the Lido has changed its natural geographical role as the city's defence against sea invasion for that of a seaside resort and residential centre of international standing. Since 1857 the Lido's low-lying, damp ground has come alive with smart beaches, shady avenues, highclass villas, luxurious hotels and elegant meeting places. Its centre of Santa Maria Elisabetta can be reached in about ten minutes by ferry from Venice. There we find a ferment of life and worldliness, the main attraction being the splendid sands of its beaches, on which stand exclusive hotels like the Excelsior which, with its Moorish style, provided an exotic thrill for the

Lido. Art Nouveau Façade (det.).

Moorish style, provided an exotic thrill for the "beau monde" in the early years of this century. This development would probably have upset Lord Byron, who came here to enjoy solitary horserides and, it is said, unobserved swims, which he would not do as a boy so that no-one could see his limp. Wagner, however, was not displeased by its new worldly character, and arrived here in a gondola at every dusk. At a time when the waves of visitors were still a phenomenon

Lido. A view.

of the future, Frederick William Rolfe, an eccentric and quarrelsome Englishman with a certain literary talent and better known as Baron Corvo, coasted past the Lido almost daily on his long and intrepid voyages.

In our own day, although maintaining intact its prerogative as a delightful garden the Lido has decidedly lost both its languid, romantic air and its noticeably fashionable nature in favour of a widespread residential character overflowing from Venice itself.

Lido. San Nicoló.

Lido. The beach.

Lido. Lagoon canals.

Canaletto. Marriage with the sea.

THINGS TO SEE

CHURCH OF SAN NICOLÒ

A 17th-century building with an unfinished façade. There was an adjoining convent of Benedictine monks. Of this earlier construction there remains the Cloister (1530) and a 14th-century wing. Inside there is a particularly interesting wooden choir with 27 stalls. Nearby are the last evocative traces of La Serenissima's defence works, represented by the former Fort of San Nicolò.

The Coastline

It can be comfortably traversed to the Alberoni at the other end by public bus, but we may rather regret that there is no longer an opportunity to do the same journey by water on a chuffing steamer that then went on to Chioggia.

Shuddering at certain town planning projects which, in the early fifties, envisaged the construction of a causeway that was to have linked the mainland at Chioggia with that at Tessera (Airport) and Puntasabbioni, passing through Pellestrina, Poveglia, the Lido and Sant'Erasmo, or a railway that reached as far as Sant'Erasmo, Vignole and the Island of Certosa, let us, before we proceed, enjoy from Santa Maria Elisabetta the splendid expanse of St Mark's Basin, hoping that we shall find ourselves here on one of those rare days when the air is transparent enough to allow a view of the soft Euganean Hills or the splendid Dolomites in the background.

Not far away our gaze encounters some highly interesting relics of Venetian history.

The Island of San Lazzaro degli Armeni was assigned in 1717 to a noble Armenian known as "Mechitar" (the Comforter), and since that time, with its library and its small museum, it has continued to be an oriental jewel in a lagoon setting.

A little further on, the Lazzaretto Vecchio (Old Lazar House) takes us back to the dark times of the plague which mowed down the population of Venice, and reminds us of the precocious sanitary intuition that led them to provide isolation in a separate place for those afflicted with the disease. After this island, proceeding along the coast elegant with small villas and burgeoning with oleanders, the lagoon spreads wide and silent, sad and solitary, but incomparably beautiful in the evening, when sunset achieves a consuming grandeur.

The population density of Santa Maria Elisabetta steadily decreases, and again grows up around the centre of Malamocco. This arose somewhat to the west of the ancient town of Metamaucus, which between 742 and 881 was the first seat of the Venetian islands' Duchy before it transferred to Rivoaltus (Rialto), and was subsequently destroyed by the terrifying tidal wave of 1106-7. It is an evocative experience to visit the small town of Malamocco, where we can find certain traces of Venetian rustic life. especially if we go all round it, following a canal which goes inland and then comes back to the lagoon.

Almost opposite, the belfry on the Island of Poveglia may remind us of the ancient poplars that used to stand there, giving rise to the Roman name Popilia, while we approach the very end of the Lido, the area known as the Alberoni, also

Views of San Lazzaro degli Armeni.

San Piero in Volta.

drawing its name from the huge trees (alberi) that stood beside an ancient fort. It is now a popular golf-links.

Continuing the line of the Lido, the Pellestrina littoral is a similar natural defensive barrier in the lagoon formation. Between the two lies the second mouth of the port, and here the sea current penetrates at a greater speed than through the other mouths because of the much-opposed Canale dei Petroli, which was extensively dredged in the sixties to allow ships of high tonnage direct access to the wharves at Marghera. The problems concerned with the industrial development that began round the lagoon in the thirties are even today far from having been settled by ideal solutions that satisfy, on the one hand, ecological requirements to guard against an increasingly evident degradation of the environment and, on the other, working people's de-

Fishing Nets.

mands for employment and enterprise opportunities.

It is clear that here too, as in the places we have visited earlier, living reality and history, progress and conservation, present and past are confused and intertwined, while the multiplicity of emotions that assail our sensibilities blends into a feeling of unease at the sense of precarious fragility suggested by this almost illusory entity called "Lagoon".

San Pietro in Volta and Pellestrina, where we can eat good fish and tasty crustaceans while enjoying a stunning view, give us a shock in the first instance by their sense of apartness, even more islanded than the places we have seen already.

Here it is nature itself that is more harsh and barren. The dwellings do not teeter in flirtatious colours or tinsel architecture but remain realistically limited by their function as they stretch in a thinning line along the narrow confines of the coastal strip, like a cane-brake bent by the wind but firmly rooted into the sand. The Pellestrina littoral undergoes the double and contrasting experience of being caressed by the lagoon on one side while the other is attacked and battered by the raging sea repelled by its mighty dykes, the "Murazzi", which are a good four kilometres long.

This gigantic work derives from the genius of the cosmographer Coronelli. He conceived the idea in 1716 but, like many a special safety measure, it was not begun until 1744 and only completed 38 years later.

The history of the Venetian Republic again overtakes us, like the incessant wind that rebounds and slides high, repelled by the shield of this enormous dyke, before

Fishing Nets.

which Goethe remained in ecstasy, leaving in his diary this still valid reflection. If Venice lives today with her islands and her canals that intersect the marshes and can be used even at times of high tide, this is entirely due to the commitment and diligence of man, and this commitment and diligence must preserve her.

There are frequent connections for the Lido which is reached in about 15 minutes.

Alight on the Lido at Santa Maria Elisabetta and, to go on to Pellestrina and Chioggia, take a Line 11 bus which uses a motor raft to cross the two harbour mouths at Alberoni and Chioggia.

The buses are so frequent that one can comfortably plan stops at Alberoni, San Pietro in Volta and Pellestrina, where there are some excellent restaurants.

Lagoon Sunset.

Chioggia and Sottomarina

O ur voyage still follows the lagoon, towards Chioggia, our last stop. In fact a public service ferry has transferred us from the Alberoni to San Pietro in Volta, and now, after having covered the whole of the Pellestrina littoral, we are aboard another ferry ready to cross the Porto di Chioggia, the Venetian lagoon's third and last opening to the sea.

But our unpredictable imagination transports us into yet other dimensions which overlap confusedly on the path of ancient memories and images faded by time.

We seem to find ourselves with quite a picturesque crowd of shipboard companions, actors and actresses, twelve altogether, a prompter, a scene shifter, a wardrobe master, eight manservants, four maidservants, two wet-nurses, youngsters of all ages, dogs, cats, monkeys, parrots, canaries, pigeons and a lamb - a veritable Noah's ark. Somewhat apart sits a youth who looks rather shy but has lively and inquisitive eyes. He observes us with curiosity, saying that his name is Carlo Goldoni and that he has sneaked on under cover of night, attracted by the company of actors and also wanting to go to Chioggia to visit his mother.

At the mouth of the port the small fishing boats known as "bragozzi", peculiar to the Adriatic, slide out with hard-working dignity, catching the first morning breeze in their ochre-coloured sails. Are they real, or a persistent dream that imposes itself on our sight, inspired by that marvellous painting by Leopoldo Robert entitled The

Chioggia. Fishing boats.

Departure of the Chioggia Fishing Fleet, seen some time ago in his studio at Palazzo Pisani in Campo Santo Stefano? This same Robert committed suicide, apparently for love of a Bonaparte girl, niece of Napoleon I. That was what George Sand said, and she knew his landlady well.

It cannot be! That would make it 1835 or soon after, whereas those scorched, derelict hulks that we see on the sandbank belong to the Genoese beaten by the Venetians, unwilling to suffer the same fate as the faithful and gallant Chioggia. The danger was undoubtedly great.

The enemy had succeeded in penetrating as far as Poveglia, destroying everything in their path, but the shrewd commanders Zeno and Pisani, using their knowledge of the lagoon shoals, finally gained the upper hand. Are we back then in the late 14th century?

A hooting siren recalls us to reality. Modern motorised fishing boats chug past us, heading out to sea.

Chioggia is situated between the lagoon and the open sea, surrounded near the mainland by rich valleys abounding in game. But like the flora and fauna of the lagoon, which vary appreciably according to the changing balance between salt sea-water and fresh river-water, it is different from other built-up areas and assumes the marked characteristics of a sea town.

It is one of the most important fishing centres, its production relying both on the Adriatic catch - progressively undermined, however, by pollution problems - and the develop-

Chioggia. Symbol of the city.

Chioggia. Colourful fishing boats.

ment of fish farming in its neighbouring wet valleys. During our crossing to Chioggia we can glimpse long skeins of rope laid as though combed onto the water, used for mussel farming and an intrinsic part of the lagoon landscape. Our first landing point is Piazzetta Vigo, where a column topped by a 12th-century Veneto-Byzantine capital surmounted by a winged lion proclaims the historical and social link with the larger city.

Leading off from here is the Corso del Popolo, the main street, a wide thoroughfare fringed like a fishbone with narrow alleys and picturesque districts.

Although Chioggia, like Venice, is a city built on water, and has very similar architecture, it has not managed to resist being taken over by motor traffic, and this inevitably creates a certain discomfort due to the coexistence of two antithetic systems.

From Ponte Vigo, adjacent to the Piazzetta of the same name, and turning our backs to the lagoon, we can admire the oldest and most typically Venetian part of the island

which runs in a fine vista along the Canal Vena, flanked by fine palaces resting over the water on their characteristic porticoes.

At the nearby Fish Market we have no hope of finding the old fishermen of yore, sucking rustic terracotta pipes, with sunburned faces and big pointed caps of red wool, but all the same we only need the flash of gilthead, mullet, bass and sardine as they are tipped out for sale on the stalls, the cheerful bargaining of the housewives and the strong smell of the briefly idle nets to recall the movement and colour of an ancient ritual, all carried out in the melodious sing-song of the Chioggia dialect.

Carlo Goldoni, who had a good ear for music, wrote it down in an unforgettable score after observing the tussles of the inhabitants while he was carrying out his job as a "cogidor", or lawyer's assistant, to the Cancelliere Criminale (Clerk of the Criminal Court), or eavesdropping on them from behind a window opposite the little church of San Francesco delle Muneghette, in the same house where lived the famous 18th century Venetian portrait painter Rosalba Carriera.

Here too the churches and the signs of devotion abound, scattered more or less everywhere through the town's urban fabric, where we can read long tracts of history from Veneto-Byzantine evidence and finds, down to the subsequent refacing operations of the 18th century.

The best example is the Cathedral, rebuilt in 1674 to a design by Baldassare Longhena after the fire that destroyed the old Duomo of Santa Maria, which was certainly already there in the 11th century, also its 13th-century bell tower alongside. Flanking the Piazza Vescovile (Bishop's Square) is a marble balustrade adorned with statues; it once lined the Canale Perotolo where the fishermen tied up their boats, and recalls picturesque hints of things utterly vanished.

A seafarers' city of ancient history and lasting tradition, Chioggia is anchored to the benefits and the contradictions of the present day by two bridges. The Ponte Lungo, constructed in stone in 1758, links it to its agricultural and industrial hinterland, while the Nuovo Ponte joins it to the Sottomarina littoral, a tourist seaside resort of primary importance.

Chioggia. Canal Vena.

Chioggia. Canale Lombardo.

Chioggia. Fish market (detail).

Bacino di Chioggia

Chioggia

Bacino Vigo

Laguna

I. S. Domenico

1 Church of S. Domenico

Canale Lombardo Esterno

Zona Portuale

Church of S. Andrea

I. di Buon Castello

Sottomarina

Veneta

Isola dei Saloni

2

Fondamenta Lungomare

Fondamenta Lungomare

Isola dei Cantieri

3 Church of S. Giacomo

C. S. Giacomo

Viale San Marco

4

Canale

Corso del Popolo

Canale Domenico

Cathedral

Isola di Unione

Viale Veneto

Canale Lombardo (Naviga.)

Ponte Lungo

Viale San Marco

Viale Padova

Laguna di Lusenzo

---

1 CHIOGGIA - CHURCH OF SAN DOMENICO

Of ancient origin, it underwent restoration at the beginning of the last century. It holds some interesting paintings, including one of Saint Paul by Carpaccio.

2 CHIOGGIA - CHURCH OF SANT'ANDREA

The Baroque refacing of the façade dates from 1743. The Veneto-Byzantine bell tower alongside dates from the 13th century. The inside is in the form of a Latin cross. On the main altar, presbytery and cupola are recent frescoes (1910-11) by the painter Cherubini, very active in Venice.

3 CHIOGGIA - CHURCH OF SAN GIACOMO

Rebuilt in the first half of the 18th century, but the façade is still unfinished. Alongside is the little 16th-century bell tower of the Church of the Transfiguration.

Chioggia. A View.

4 CHIOGGIA - CATHEDRAL

The rebuilding of the old cathedral of Santa Maria after the fire of 1673 was undertaken after Baldassare Longhena's design and brought to completion in 1674, though leaving the façade unfinished. Beside it is the typical Venetian form of 14th-century bell tower.
The splendid, finely proportioned interior is rich in paintings, stuccoes and marble inlays.

Punta Sabbioni, Cavallino, Jesolo

A s we were crossing the short stretch of sea that separates the island of Sant'Erasmo from the point of San Nicolò del Lido, leaving the massive whitish fort of Sant'Andrea on our right, our attention was drawn to the harbour mouth, and for a moment we seemed to

Jesolo lighthouse.

economic and social development in tourism and for its natural charm. Via Fausta, the straight motor road linking Punta Sabbioni and the Cavallino littoral, is practically a demarcation line between holiday life on the camping sites among the dunes, the cluster pines

see, against the light, golden glint of the Bucintoro, slow and stately as a marsh bird, its oars moving in wide cadence, on its way to the Wedding to the Sea. In those days the sea bed was deeper than it is now, and the sea met the lagoon in different ways. Here, probably more than elsewhere, there is much evidence of the work systematically undertaken by the Venetian Republic to protect the survival of the lagoon's ecosystem.

The names Punta Sabbioni (sandy point), Treporti (three ports), Rio Grande (big river) and Porto Secco (dry dock) are vividly indicative of the coast's evolution both by natural causes and at the hand of man. Treporti records the existence of three harbour mouths in the area, while Punta Sabbioni indicates the immense build-up of sand over the years, retained even more by the long dykes constructed at the beginning of this century.

We land at Punta Sabbioni, at the end of an interesting "peninsula" running as far as the bank of the River Sile, affording protection against the sea on one side and enclosing a vast expanse of lagoon on the other. These two factors have been important both for its recent

and the regular lines of poplars on its shore, and a view of country life running down gradually on the lonely lagoon side intersected by fishing valleys.

Anyone staying in this area finds himself in the happy situation of being faced with a varied range of choice between the sea, the lagoon, the countryside, and the rapid proximity of Venice or Burano and Torcello, which may be reached by a direct line from the Treporti landing stage. Not to mention that we are now on terrafirma and the use of a car will take us into nearby Jesolo and all the surrounding land of extreme touristic and historical appeal. Adhering to the acquatic nature of this itinerary, at Lio Piccolo, not far from Punta Sabbioni, we find a welcoming little harbour for pleasure craft, from which one can set out on all the trips hitherto described, and possibly others no less fascinating and evocative. For example, one could take a short detour and go up the canal skirting the old salt flats of San Felice as far as the tiny isolated settlement of Lio Grande, embedded in a landscape composed of the typical features of a lagoon nature park; from its quiet

Jesolo beach.

Jesolo. Beach views.

and sunny expanse it is not infrequent to see a flight of birds take off, one of the various ornithological species that live or overwinter in these waters. Alternatively, one could follow the sinuous Canale di Pordelio, which flows parallel to the motor road and arrives among shoals, large valley houses and fishermen's huts, up to the charming village of Cavallino. At the end, a small manmade cut takes us to the Cavallino Basin, constructed to enable vessels to navigate the unequal water levels between the lagoon and the River Sile; this in fact runs in the former bed of the Piave, which was diverted further east around the second half of the 17th century.

Thus we once again find ourselves overwhelmed by the impressive work put into effect by the government of La Serenissima in past centuries, which enables us even now to enjoy one of the largest natural parks linked to a historic city.

Passage from the lagoon to a river environment cannot fail to arouse immediately new and stunning sensations... But this is obviously another adventure.

The town of Jesolo has an age-old history, dating from its foundation on the island of Equilium to its present structure. Jesolo Litorale is a modern beach area stretching over 15 km., with 411 hotels, 7 camping areas, 5217 apartments and various other types of tourist facilities. Venice, which can be reached by motor ship from Punta Sabbioni, is the nearest cultural centre of world-wide importance.

Views of the North Lagoon.

Text: Enrico Ricciardi
Graphic Design: Storti Edizioni srl
Photography: Archivio Storti Edizioni
                Cameraphoto immagini

Storti Edizioni srl
Via Brianza, 9/c
30030 Oriago di Mira - VENEZIA

Tel. 041.5659057 / 041.5659058
Fax 041.5631157
E-mail: edstort@tin.it
Internet: www.stortiedizioni.com